Charles Darwin
and Evolution

Yoming S. Lin

PowerKiDS
press.
New York

To Mom, Dad, and Mindy, with love

Published in 2012 by The Rosen Publishing Group, Inc.
29 East 21st Street, New York, NY 10010

First Edition

Editor: Amelie von Zumbusch
Book Design: Greg Tucker

Photo Credits: Cover (Darwin), p. 20 (top left) Bob Thomas/Popperfoto/Getty Images; cover (inset), pp. 5, 9 (top, bottom), 11 (top, bottom), 13, 16, 19, 20 (top right) Shutterstock.com; pp. 4, 20 (bottom left) Mansell/Time & Life Pictures/Getty Images; p. 6 Joseph Wright of Derby/Getty Images; pp. 7, 10, 15 Hulton Archive/Getty Images; p. 8 Kilburn/Hulton Archive/Getty Images; p. 12 © www.iStockphoto.com/Kristian Larsen; p. 14 Chris Sharp/Getty Images; p. 17 Kenneth Garrett/ Getty Images; p. 18 Julia Margaret Cameron/Getty Images; p. 21 iStockphoto/Thinkstock.

Library of Congress Cataloging-in-Publication Data

Lin, Yoming S.
 Charles Darwin and evolution / by Yoming S. Lin. — 1st ed.
    p. cm. — (Eureka!)
 Includes index.
 ISBN 978-1-4488-5031-0 (library binding)
 1. Darwin, Charles, 1809-1882—Juvenile literature. 2. Evolution (Biology)—History—Juvenile literature. 3. Naturalists—England—Biography—Juvenile literature. I. Title.
 QH31.D2L496 2012
 576.8'2092—dc22
 [B]
                        2011004470

Manufactured in the United States of America

CPSIA Compliance Information: Batch #WS11PK: For Further Information contact Rosen Publishing, New York, New York at 1-800-237-9932

Contents

Darwin's World

Have you ever wondered where all the kinds of things living on Earth came from? Charles Darwin did. Darwin was an English scientist. He was born over 200 years ago.

Through his travels to faraway lands and years of hard work, Darwin came up with an important scientific **theory**. In science, a theory is an

Charles Darwin based his theory of evolution on what he saw in nature. It took him many years to fully develop the theory.

Giraffes' long necks make it easy for them to eat leaves at the tops of trees. Darwin's theory explains how animals with useful features like this evolve.

explanation that most scientists agree on of why or how things happen in the natural world. Darwin came up with a theory of **evolution**. Darwin's theory explains how living things evolve, or change over long periods of time, to become new kinds of plants and animals. His theory changed the way scientists look at our world.

A Childhood Spent in Nature

Charles Robert Darwin was born in Shrewsbury, England, in 1809. He came from a rich family. His parents were Susannah and Robert Darwin. Robert Darwin was a successful doctor.

Charles Darwin was shy as a boy. He liked spending time outdoors studying plants and collecting beetles. Sadly, his mother

One of Charles Darwin's grandfathers was Erasmus Darwin, seen here. Erasmus Darwin was a well-known doctor, writer, and scientist.

This drawing shows Charles Darwin and his younger sister, Emily Catherine, as children. Charles had four sisters and one brother.

died when he was eight years old. After that, his older sisters helped take care of him.

In 1817, young Charles started going to the Shrewsbury School. There, he learned geography, history, and Latin. He did not find school very interesting. Robert Darwin was upset that his son was not a better student.

In 1825, Darwin began taking classes at the **University** of Edinburgh, in Edinburgh, Scotland. He studied medicine but decided not to become a doctor.

Darwin left Edinburgh to study at the University of Cambridge in Cambridge, England. One subject he studied there was **geology**. Geology is the study of the rocks that make up Earth. In August 1831,

Adam Sedgwick was among the first modern geologists. Though he had taught Darwin, Sedgwick did not agree with his theory of evolution.

Top: Darwin studied at Christ's College, Cambridge, seen here. *Bottom*: You can see rock layers on this hillside. The different layers formed at different times.

Darwin and his geology teacher Adam Sedgwick visited Wales to study rock **layers**, or levels.

When he got home from Wales, Darwin got a letter asking him to travel around the world on a ship called the HMS *Beagle*. His job would be to study nature and geology. He happily agreed to go.

On the *Beagle*, Darwin read the works of geologist Charles Lyell. Lyell believed that Earth's rocks had been shaped slowly over time. Darwin wondered if living things might also change over time.

Wherever the *Beagle* stopped, Darwin studied **fossils** in the rocks. Fossils are the remains of living things. Darwin saw fossils of plants and animals that no longer existed. This showed that **species**,

This drawing shows the *Beagle* sailing through the Strait of Magellan, at the southern tip of South America. The *Beagle* spent a lot of time in South America.

or kinds of living things, can die out.

Darwin studied living animals, too. One place the *Beagle* stopped was the Galápagos Islands, off of South America. There, Darwin collected examples of several species of birds called finches. Each island was home to a different mix of finch species.

Darwin saw iguanas (top) and tortoises (bottom) in the Galápagos Islands. Many of the animals found on these islands live nowhere else.

11

Darwin's Biggest Idea

After returning to England, Darwin studied the finches he had collected. Each species' bill was just the right shape for the food it ate. He thought that the finches had **adapted**, or changed, to suit the foods found in the islands where they lived.

How did these changes happen, though? Darwin noted that animals of

This bird is a small tree finch. Small tree finches eat mostly insects. Their beaks are a good shape for catching insects.

one species could have different **traits**, or features. He realized that animals with useful traits would live longer and have more babies. Their babies would have the same traits. Animals with less useful traits would die younger and

Large ground finch beaks are good for breaking open hard seeds. You can see how different this large ground finch's beak is from that of the small tree finch on page 12.

have fewer babies. Their traits would die out over time. In time, the animals with useful traits would become a new species. Darwin called this process **natural selection**.

Darwin spent years thinking about natural selection. He wanted to have strong arguments. He knew that the idea of evolution through natural selection would upset people who believed that every species had been created at the beginning of time.

During these years, Darwin suffered from health problems. He was busy with his

Darwin lived in Down House from 1842 on. The house is in the village of Downe in the county of Kent. Darwin liked walking in the gardens there.

family, too. He married Emma Wedgwood in 1839. They had 10 children and were loving parents. In 1851, their 10-year-old daughter, Annie, became sick and died. Darwin and his wife were very sad.

Darwin still wanted to share his work on evolution with the world, though. He decided to write a book explaining his theory.

This picture of Emma Wedgwood Darwin was taken in her later years. Charles Darwin was close to his wife and talked about his ideas with her.

This young ape is a chimpanzee. As you can see, chimpanzees look a bit like people. This is because they are the species most closely related to people.

Darwin called his book on evolution *On the Origin of Species*. When it came out in 1859, he had been thinking about evolution for 20 years.

In 1871, Darwin came out with a book called *The Descent of Man*. In the book, he argued that people, like all other living things, went through evolution. He said that

This is the skull, or the bones that form the head, of a species called *Homo erectus*. It was an early relative of people that was more closely related to apes.

people were closely related to apes, monkeys, and other **primates**. Over a long period of time, certain primates evolved into people.

Some people, including some church leaders, were upset with Darwin's ideas on evolution. Most scientists accepted his ideas pretty quickly, though.

Darwin the Great Scientist

After Darwin's books on evolution came out, he continued to write scientific books. One book was about **emotions**, or feelings, in animals and people. Another was about plants that eat insects. He also wrote about plant movement and flowers. Darwin died in 1882. He was buried in Westminster Abbey, which is England's most famous church. In the years since Darwin died,

In his later years, Darwin was a very respected scientist. He continued to study nature and spent time with his family.

Parents pass DNA down to their children. This is the reason that people with the same parents, such as this brother and sister, look a bit alike.

scientists have learned more about how evolution works. We now know that living things pass on their traits in their DNA. DNA is a special code that spells out the traits living things have. Though we keep learning more about evolution, our understanding is still based on Darwin's theory.

Timeline

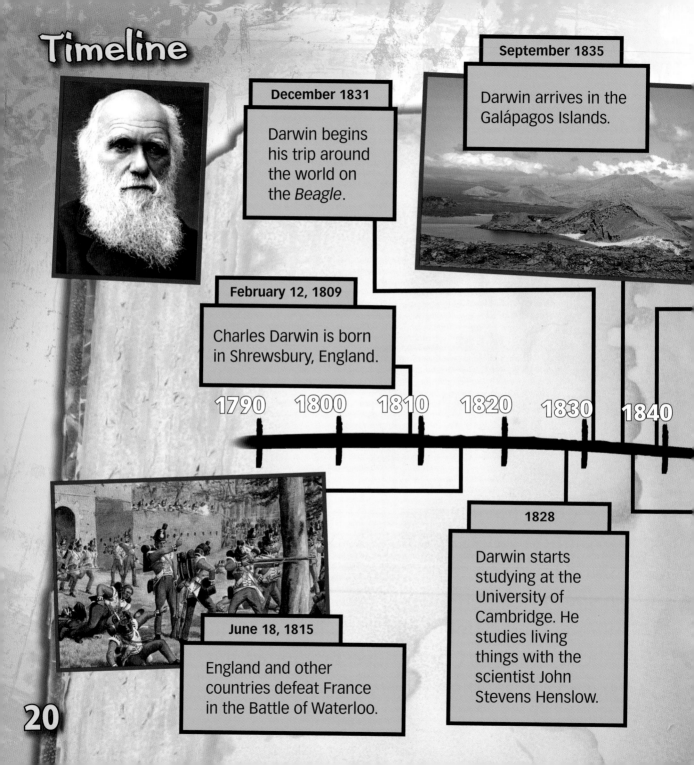

December 1831

Darwin begins his trip around the world on the *Beagle*.

September 1835

Darwin arrives in the Galápagos Islands.

February 12, 1809

Charles Darwin is born in Shrewsbury, England.

1790   1800   1810   1820   1830   1840

1828

Darwin starts studying at the University of Cambridge. He studies living things with the scientist John Stevens Henslow.

June 18, 1815

England and other countries defeat France in the Battle of Waterloo.

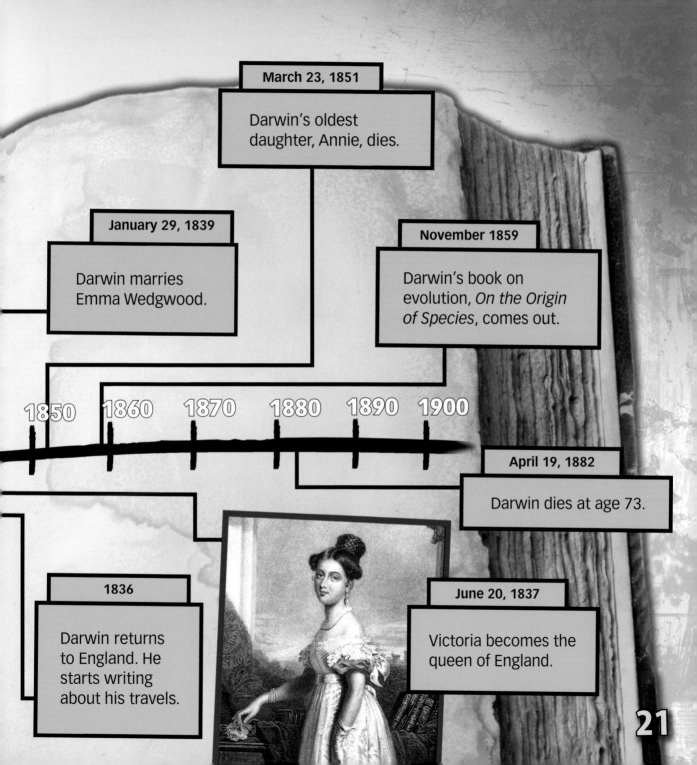

March 23, 1851

Darwin's oldest daughter, Annie, dies.

January 29, 1839

Darwin marries Emma Wedgwood.

November 1859

Darwin's book on evolution, *On the Origin of Species*, comes out.

1850 1860 1870 1880 1890 1900

April 19, 1882

Darwin dies at age 73.

1836

Darwin returns to England. He starts writing about his travels.

June 20, 1837

Victoria becomes the queen of England.

Inside the Science

1. Any remains or traces of living things from the past are fossils. A piece of bone that has turned into rock and a footprint that is millions of years old are both fossils. Fossils give us clues to what living things were like in the past.

2. The layers in Earth's rocks formed at different times. The lower layers formed first. The layers above them formed later. Studying these layers can teach us about Earth's past.

3. If animals of one species live in different places and do not mix much, they may evolve into different species over time. For example, Harris's antelope squirrels evolved on the south side of Arizona's Grand Canyon, while white-tailed antelope squirrels evolved on the canyon's north side.

4. Evolution causes new families, or groups of species, to form. Old World monkeys live in Europe, Asia, and Africa. New World monkeys live in North America and South America. Some species of New World monkeys can hang from their tails. No Old World monkeys have this trait.

5. Scientists have mapped out the DNA of many animals. These maps show that all living things are related and share a lot of the same DNA code.

Glossary

adapted (uh-DAP-ted) Changed to fit new conditions.

emotions (ih-MOH-shunz) Feelings.

evolution (eh-vuh-LOO-shun) Changing over many years.

fossils (FO-sulz) The hardened remains of dead animals or plants.

geology (jee-AH-luh-jee) The study of rocks and the formation of the crust of Earth.

layers (LAY-erz) Thicknesses of something.

natural selection (NA-chuh-rul suh-LEK-shun) What steers evolution.

primates (PRY-mayts) A group of animals that includes monkeys, gorillas, and people.

species (SPEE-sheez) One kind of living thing. All people are one species.

theory (THEE-uh-ree) An idea or group of ideas that tries to explain something.

traits (TRAYTS) Features that make an individual special.

university (yoo-neh-VER-seh-tee) A school one goes to after high school.

Index

Web Sites

Due to the changing nature of Internet links, PowerKids Press has developed an online list of Web sites related to the subject of this book. This site is updated regularly. Please use this link to access the list:
www.powerkidslinks.com/eure/darwin/